# KAYAK FISHING MADE EASY

## A Practical Sea Angler's Guide for Catching Your Favorite Big Fish from a Kayak

By Scott Parsons

**Disclaimer:** The information within this book is intended as reference materials only and not as substitute for professional advice. Information contained herein is intended to give you the tools to make informed decisions about your kayaking skills and ability to fish from a kayak. Every reasonable effort has been made to ensure that the material in this book "Kayak fishing made easy" is true, correct, complete and appropriate at the time of writing.

The Author and Publisher has strived to be as accurate and complete as possible in the creation of this book, notwithstanding the fact that he does not warrant or represent at any time that the contents within are accurate due to the rapidly changing nature of the subject and the Internet (third party website links). Nevertheless the Author and Publisher assume no liability or responsibility for any omission or error, for damage or injury to you or other persons arising from the use of this material. Reliance upon information contained in this material is solely at the reader's own risk.

Any perceived slights of specific persons, peoples, or organizations are unintentional. This book is not intended as a substitute for the medical advice of physicians. Like any other recreational activity, kayak fishing poses some inherent risk. The Author and Publisher advice readers to take full responsibility for their safety and know their limits. Before practicing the skills described in this book, be sure that your equipment is well maintained, and do not take risks beyond your level of experience, aptitude, training and comfort level.

First Printing, 2013 - Printed in the United States of America

*"The attraction of angling for all the ages of man, from the cradle to the grave, lies in its uncertainty."*

# TABLE OF CONTENTS

# INTRODUCTION

The line goes taut and the rod bends to the water! Line screams out of the reel and the big game ocean monster leaps out of the water. The contest is on between the angler and the fish and only with practice and experience will the angler be the victor.

This scenario has repeated itself over thousands of years in all the waters of the earth. Fishing has been a means of survival for countless people and is one of the earliest human activities. Cultures from Polynesia to the Arctic, Mediterranean to Caribbean and every place in between have looked to the ocean for their food source.

For hundreds of years, however, fishing has also been a pastime practiced and enjoyed by many people as much as it has been a way to provide food for the family. In fact, an avid fisherman, Izaak Walton, wrote a book entitled "*The Compleat Angler; or, The Contemplative Man's Recreation*" almost 400 years ago!

Today, millions of sport fishermen, both male and female, take part in the art and sport of fishing, some for leisure and others for the excitement. They cast their lines in fresh and saltwater, from the shore or from boats. The boats themselves come in many different sizes such as large fishing charter yachts, average sized motor boats or smaller dinghies and even canoes and kayaks.

This work describes **salt water fishing from a kayak** and the **special skills and equipment required to remain safe and be successful**. A working knowledge of fishing is assumed so the content focuses on how fishing from a kayak is different from any other method. By the end, you too will appreciate the benefits unique to kayak fishing and be ready to give it a try!

Beginning with some background regarding kayaking in general, the text moves on to suggestions for **selecting the most appropriate kayak and equipment** for the type of fishing you intend to pursue in salt water. From there, you will learn **how to outfit the kayak** properly for having your bait, tackle and other fishing gear at hand and secure. **Methods for anchoring the kayak** will help you stay in position to get the most out of a honey hole.

Safety is always a major consideration when going out on the water so advice is provided for **self-rescue and other safety measures**. Different conditions exist throughout the year and the ways to adjust for that are included.

Basic **kayak paddling techniques** are explained and demonstrated and related to a variety of fishing styles. **How to fight and land** the big ones from the ocean depths is discussed and the steps to **preparing for a fishing trip** are explained.

Enjoy reading and watching the video links and you'll be ready to put your newfound knowledge to the test on the open seas!

# CHAPTER 1 – BEFORE YOU START

## Benefits of Kayak Fishing

**F**or most people, the decision to use a kayak for fishing comes after being a successful angler. In other words, the skill for fishing has been developed but the way to get to the fish is being changed. There are several basic **reasons that people switch to or add kayaks to their fishing routine**.

- First, kayaks are much ***easier to transport and store*** than other boats.

- That leads to the next advantage which is ***cost***. A kayak is much less expensive than any type of motor boat to begin with and it does not require much maintenance or expensive gasoline to propel it. Registration fees and permits may also be much cheaper.

- For the avid fisherman, however, the greatest advantage of a kayak is ***stealth***. There is less of a shadow, no noisy motor and the ability to move into very shallow water.

While those three points are all valid, there is also the likelihood that you truly want to experience the peace and quiet that fishing from a kayak provides or the added thrill of being virtually in the fish's element hunting and fighting him. There is nothing more elemental than being on the water in a small craft and feeling the enormity of nature all around you.

# Physical Demands of Kayak Fishing

**R**ecreational kayaking is not terribly demanding, but since it may involve more exercise than you are used to or situations that can create a shock to your system such as falling into cold water, talking to your doctor about potential health risks is a good idea. A generally good level of physical fitness enables you to paddle without too much exertion and leaves you with the strength and energy to actually fish.

Contrary to what many people believe, the arms and shoulders are not the keys to good paddling. The ***core muscles*** should perform most of the work as you rotate side to side for a powerful stroke. These muscles include the abdominals, hips and lower back and are also responsible for posture and stability. There are exercises that can build up the core muscles and basic stretches to limber your body up for maximum flexibility before hitting the water. The shoulders and arms need strength for fighting and landing a big fish.

***Cardio-respiratory fitness*** relates to endurance as much as overall strength does, if not more. The physical demands on the body require a good blood oxygen supply so the ability to breath smoothly through exertion without raising the heart rate enables you to perform well without developing cramps or exhaustion. Cross training provides the opportunity to address each of the muscle groups and increase cardio fitness. Swimming is an excellent activity because of the focus on the core as well as other muscles, stretching for flexibility and controlled breathing at a faster rate. Before heading out on the water, it is a good idea to warm up by stretching each muscle group starting from your head and progressing all the way down to your feet. Look in Appendices for a list of warming up and cooling down exercises.

***Proper nutrition and*** adequate ***hydration*** are also important elements for general fitness. Snacking occasionally as well as eating a balanced lunch helps keep the body's chemical balance in line and drinking plenty of water, a liter every two hours, keeps you awake and alert.

# A Word of Advice

Although kayaking is very popular and not too hard to master, it is a water sport and requires a good degree of common sense and logic. You need to face a few facts before you invest any time or money in buying equipment. You have to be able to swim and cannot be afraid of getting dumped into the water. Unlike fishing from a power boat, a kayak virtually guarantees that you will 'turtle' or tip over at least once, but probably a lot more. If you are prone to panic, kayaking is probably not a good idea nor is it if you do not realize and respect the power of the water and the potential strength of the fish.

To ensure a good experience, the best course of action is to take lessons from an approved, licensed kayaking instructor. This will provide you with the basics of kayaking, especially the safety and self-rescue techniques that may mean the difference between life and death. Once you try kayaking, it will probably become your favorite activity next to fishing, so combining the two will only make sense.

Joining a local kayak fishing club or a division of a larger organization can also provide you with many tips based on the combined experience of the members and the opportunity to join others as you get used to fishing by kayak. Your interest may blossom into a passion and you will be interested in participating in a tournament.

Many opportunities exist for the kayak fisherman so it's time to get started learning how it works!

# CHAPTER 2 – CHOOSING THE RIGHT EQUIPMENT

## Which Kayak is Best for You

### *Singles*

**F**or every kayak, there are people who love it and those who hate it. It's hard to tell someone else what is 'best' because each model from every manufacturer has a different feel and no two people will react the same way to it. Six basic questions will lead you towards making the best choice for yourself.

1. ***What are your personal physical requirements?***

   If you are tall or short, husky or trim, there will be different styles that fit you better.

2. ***How do you plan on transporting the kayak?***

   Hauling a kayak is not too difficult when using the bed of a pick-up truck, an SUV or a trailer, but there could be problems if you have to lift one onto the top of a vehicle. Just keep the weight of the kayak and your strength in mind, especially if you plan on going out alone.

3. ***What is your plan for the fish you catch?***

   If you are strictly 'catch and release', then storage is not much of a concern. If, on the other hand, you like to bring home the day's catch, space will be needed to store those fish. Near shore and far off shore fishing sites require slightly different equipment for the serious kayaker, but for beginners, basic models of sea fishing kayaks are adequate and not as high-priced as some fancier models.

4. *What are your fishing methods?*

Depending on your preferences, different kayaks will offer greater or lesser flexibility. If you like to use live bait, storage and easy access are an issue. Dead fish bait poses other issues and lures still others. Fly fishing, casting, free lining and dropping and dragging are each performed better from some kayaks as opposed to others, so advice from a knowledgeable salesperson and experienced sea kayak fishermen can help narrow down the choices. The outfitting and rigging of the kayak are based on particular styles and equipment choices, so again, until you get some experience and make some general decisions, a basic model kayak is the best way to start.

5. *Where do you intend to fish?*

The first consideration here is whether or not you can drive directly to a launch site or if you have to carry the kayak and gear to a remote spot. The next question concerns the type of water – is it a relatively calm area or wide open and subject to waves and surf? Longer kayaks are better suited for open water while shorter models work well in estuaries, on flats or other less turbulent areas.

6. *Which style kayak do you prefer?*

There are ***sit in kayaks*** (SIK) and ***sit on top kayaks*** (SOT). For someone new to kayaking, the SIK probably comes to mind. You picture arctic fishermen bundled up in sealskin fishing or hunting for seal. The SOT looks more like a surfboard with molded depressions for your seat and legs with scupper holes to allow water to drain easily. There are advantages and disadvantages to both, and either style is suitable for different purposes.

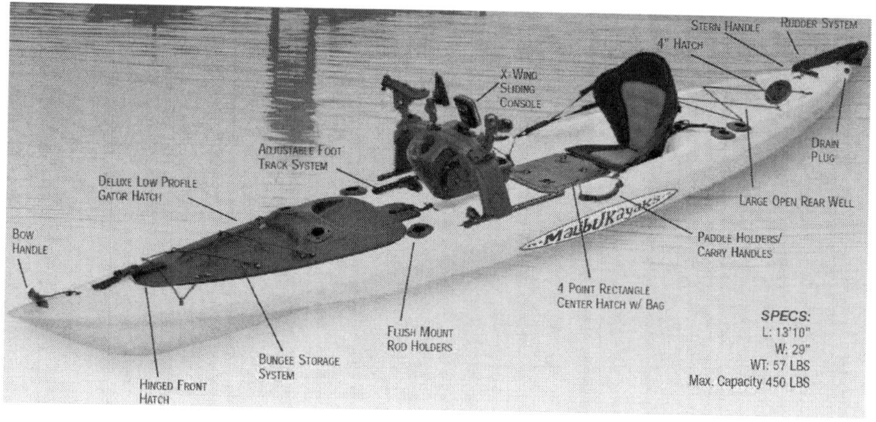


***Stability*** is a key factor in choosing between a SIK and SOT. Sit ins are usually more stable, but sit on tops are made a little wider to compensate for the higher center of gravity. They are also easier to get onto and off of in shallow water if you decide to wade and there is better range of motion. Sitting side saddle is a popular position in which your feet are over the side or on the bottom providing support and stability as you cast and fight to land a fish. Straddling or standing up on an SOT kayak are also possibilities.

***Speed*** is a factor in the sense that you may want to fish well offshore and have to cover greater distances than if you stick closer to shore in a bay or inlet. Longer, narrower craft are faster but you may not want to give up the stability of a shorter, wider kayak. Manoeuvrability is also an issue. A longer kayak may be more useful in some situations, but the length has a negative impact on the ability to move easily around obstacles.

The answers to these questions do not provide an automatic solution for choosing the best kayak. The pros and cons of each situation need to be examined and an excellent way to do that is to go to an outfitter and try several models. Also, visit a variety of sporting goods stores – big names and privately owned. Ask lots of questions and try to observe as many different set ups as possible.

## *Doubles*

Another situation that requires consideration is whether or not you are interested in a tandem or two-person kayak. As with everything else, there are pros and cons. A tandem kayak obviously has to be larger. Older tandem kayaks do not perform well with only one paddler, but newer kayaks designed to be used as a tandem or solo craft don't have the storage capacity or convenience of the location of fixed equipment.

For two kayakers to fish together, two separate kayaks may be the best choice but other circumstances point to the tandem as being more practical.

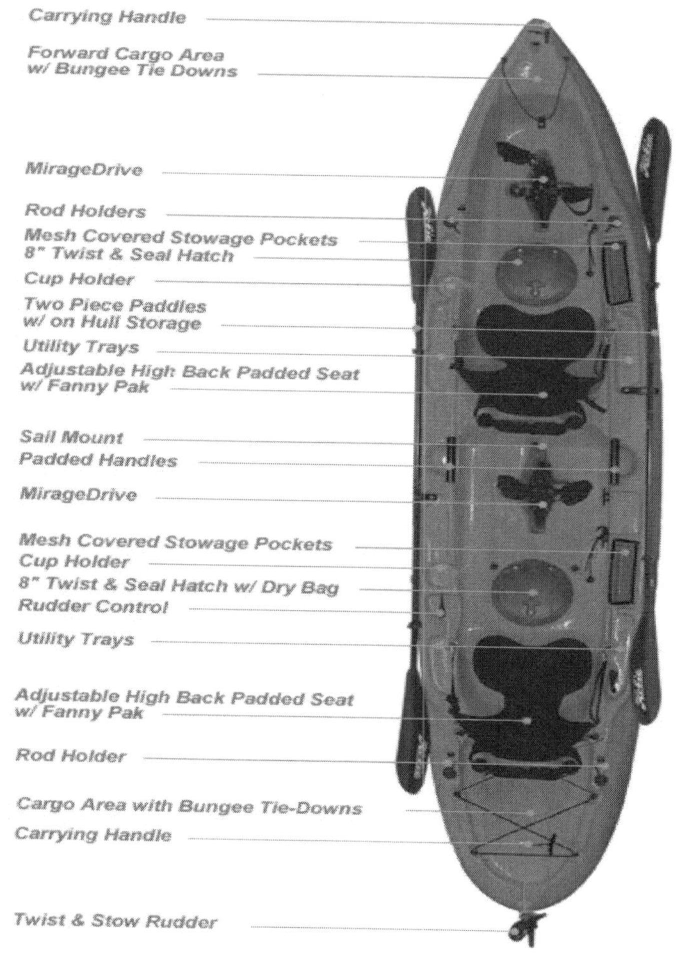

Advantages of the tandem kayak include the ability of one person to stand and spot fish while the other paddles or keeps the kayak in position and the added size makes them a bit more stable.

Two paddlers can cover more distance in a tandem or one can rest while the other paddles. Many different models are available featuring numerous combinations of length, width and storage capacity so it is important to see as many as possible and get information from the internet and other kayak fishermen.

The greatest advantage of the tandem fishing kayak is for a beginner to go out on the water with a more experienced person. The beginner can learn the basics safely and gain knowledge about the process before selecting his own kayak and gear. This is also a perfect solution for enabling a physically challenged person to fish – the other person takes care of loading, paddling and handling the gear so the second person can simply enjoy being on the water and fishing.

## *Pedals*

Pedals are an option available on many makes of kayaks. Some fishermen find these to be advantageous because both hands are free to take care of fishing and there is no need to repeatedly pick up and put down a paddle and pedaling is less tiring. It is always wise to carry a spare paddle just in case, though.

Some models have pedals that work like flippers and others use a cycling motion. The pedal motion is considered to be less efficient than the rotational or cycling drive because of the laws of momentum. The continuous pedaling motion is also easier on the legs than the flippers. A rudder that has a hand control helps keep the kayak moving in a straight line. Other than that, however, maneuvering a pedal-type kayak is more difficult and width is added for stability which may be jeopardized because the feet are higher up and closer to the center line than they are when you paddle.

For a buyer's guide on choosing a kayak please visit:
paddling.com/gear/category/kayaks

A variety of companies manufacture kayaks that are suited for salt water fishing. Among the most commonly recommended names are the *Ocean Kayak Prowler 15 Angler Edition*, *the Wilderness Systems Tarpon 120 Angler*, *the Cobra Navigator* and *the Hobie Mirage Pro Angler 14*. These kayaks are specifically outfitted for fishing and contain built in tank wells, built in rod holders, cup holders, special seats and a variety of different features that may or may not be of interest to every fisherman. Starting out, a middle range kayak from any of these manufacturers is sufficient until you learn what you like and don't like and can choose the kayak that has exactly what you are interested in.

Some anglers enjoy the DIY projects that enable them to add the exact equipment they want to their kayak. There are plenty of stripped down models perfect for the DIYer, but you have to be handy and check that your add ons are not significantly more expensive than what you would pay for an already outfitted kayak.

# The Right PFD – Personal Floatation Device

Next to the actual kayak, the most important piece of equipment you need to buy is the PFD or life vest. No one should ever be out on the water without wearing a floatation device because unexpected swims, especially far from shore, can prove to be too much for even a top swimmer.

*Type III floatation devices* are the ones most commonly used by kayakers. They provide three key features:

**Good fit**: The device should fit snugly but without binding you, and not ride up your back. Some are made with larger openings at the arm pit and neck so they don't interfere with the range of motion of a paddler. For fishing, there are special pockets and loops to carry or attach equipment.

**Buoyancy**: They are rated by body weight, so it is important to know yours and check the labels. Size does not really matter as long as the adjustable straps can fasten and provide a good fit. New floatation material is thinner so less is needed.

**Visibility**: A kayak that is low on the water line is difficult to see. The paddler needs to wear a brightly colored PFD for daytime but also have reflective strips for foggy or darkening conditions. An emergency strobe light that can be clipped to the shoulder is also available.

# Selecting the Correct Paddle

There are almost as many types of paddles as there are kayaks and the same rules apply for selecting the 'best' one for you. As a beginner to kayaking, any standard paddle fit to your height would do fine, but as you advance in your skills, a high end paddle can account for greater ease and comfort while paddling. A number of considerations come into play when looking at paddles.

- ***Blade shape***: An asymmetrical blade is better for use with a kayak because of the angle at which the blade is held. This shape creates a more even pressure on the top and bottom of the blade which allows for a more efficient stroke that is less fatiguing. Along with the asymmetry of the blade, the width and length play different roles for 'low' and 'high' angle paddlers. A shorter, wider blade is more efficient for a high angle paddler while a longer, narrower blade works better for low angle paddlers.

- ***Material used***: A variety of materials is used for making paddles for added strength or lighter weight. The basic aluminum shaft with plastic blades is durable and functional, even if it isn't the lightest paddle available. After you develop your paddling skills and are determined to improve the kayak fishing experience, a higher end paddle may be a good investment. The next lightest composition is a combination of a fiberglass shaft and blade or a blade made of carbon- reinforced nylon. The lightest paddle is made of all carbon fiber. Some of the most expensive paddles have blades with floatation foam in them to make the blade easy to bring out of the water on each stroke.

- ***Shaft length***: Your height is the primary factor in determining the length of the paddle you should use and paddling style is another. High angle paddlers do better with a shorter paddle (230 cm) whereas low angle paddlers need more length (240cm). Straight shafts are also preferred over bent shafts because of the frequency of putting down and picking up the paddle while fishing.

- ***Feathering***: This refers to the degree to which the blades are offset to make a strong stroke but lower wind resistance on the upside blade. This is a benefit for long distance paddling or dealing with windy conditions. The amount of feathering is a personal preference so experimentation is the best way to determine what is right for you.

# The Best Dressed Fisherman is the One Who is Prepared

You are certainly not trying to win a fashion prize, but you definitely want to be dressed appropriately for the conditions of the water and weather. Unless you plan to fish only in tropical waters where the biggest concern is sunburn, an awareness of the effects of cold water is necessary. *Hypothermia* – losing body heat due to the cold – can be life threatening and a warm sunny day does not mean you can't get cold. Water stays much colder than the land during the spring and even early summer, so it may not take long for the effects of hypothermia to prevent you from being able to rescue yourself. An unexpected dip and wet clothes are also a problem in cooler weather.

**Layering** is the best way to be prepared for the varying conditions that occur throughout the day. A full dry suit is that keeps water out and body heat in makes the most sense for early spring or late fall fishing. Other than that, you should start with a wicking layer to keep moisture off your skin and add layers for insulation. It is better to take something off than to wish you had more to put on. An outer layer for wind and spray keeps the elements out while letting air circulate. There are specially made dry tops that have secure wrist, neck and waist closures and can be used with waders. Waders, contrary to popular belief, can be kept water tight to they do not fill up if you are tipped over. Spray jackets and pants that are breathable can keep the elements at bay and fit over other layers that can be added or removed. A hat and gloves for either cold or sun should be carried along if not worn and some type of secure footwear is recommended for warmth and the protection of your feet if you find yourself wading or walking.

Carrying a dry bag with a change of clothes and extra gloves and socks should get you through most situations, but it is also a good idea to have an emergency blanket and chemical hand and foot warmers in the event of a beaching in an isolated area.

As with any of the equipment you need for kayaking, outfitters, sporting goods stores and online sources can provide you with information about the latest advancements in materials and styles of protective clothing.

And of course, don't forget to wear a PFD!

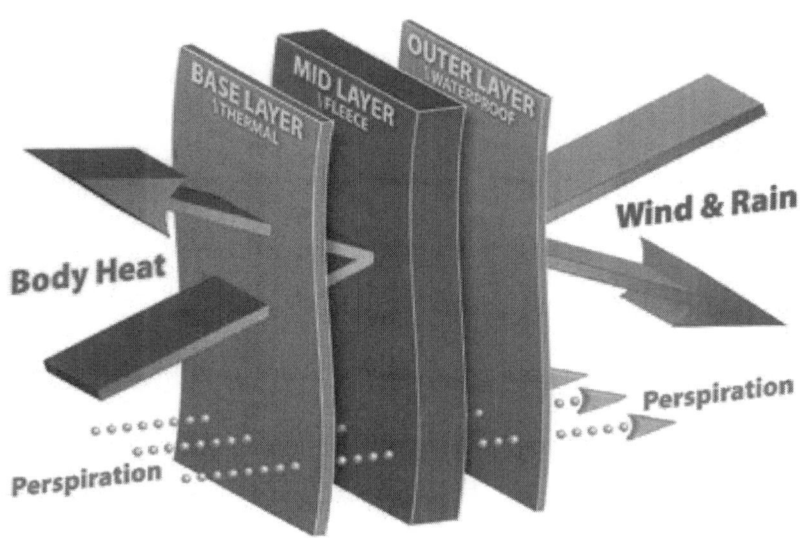

NRS

# CHAPTER 3 – FISHING GEAR FOR THE KAYAK

## The Basics and Beyond

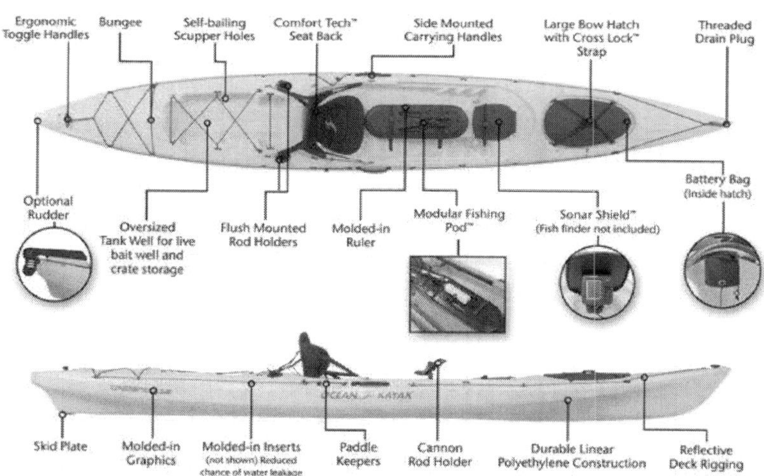


Think back to lazy summer days when a boy tied a string on a stick and spent hours on the river bank fishing. He was happy with the barest minimum of equipment. Most people use more than that, but it still does not have to be a big production. At the absolute minimum, a ***kayak fisherman needs very few things***:

A simple plastic or wooden crate with two short pieces of PVC pipe tied into the corners as rod holders and storage space

- A PFD (required by law)
- A spare paddle (two pieces are the most convenient)
- An emergency whistle or horn (required by law)
- A fishing rod (fly or reel)
- A set of lures or live bait
- Lip grippers and gloves
- A net
- A water bottle
- A hat and sunscreen

If that were truly all you need, though, there wouldn't be a billion dollar fishing industry supplying all types of gadgets and gewgaws. So what are some of these ***other types of equipment that make kayak fishing much more relaxing and rewarding***?

1. **Hardware**: Many of these items are for repairs or replacements, but a significant number have special purposes. For example, you can buy one of many types of paddle leashes or paddle clips, paddle splash guards to keep water from running down the shaft onto your hands between strokes, sails and sail installation kits and other personal gear like water bottles, back packs and summer shower bags. Live bait wells powered by batteries are another option along with regular bait pails, but dragging bait or stringing fish is not a good idea in the ocean due to predators.

2. **Hatches**: To add more storage space, you can cut through the top deck of the kayak and install a hatch to seal the compartment shut. This may be for bait tanks, fish storage or dry storage bags and cases.

3. **Lights**: Boating regulations require a 360°visible light for any craft on the water before dawn, after dusk or in any low-light situation. Complete running light packages are available as well as emergency lights, flashers and head lamps.

4. **Individual electronic accessories** such as fish finders, GPS units and sonar may be battery operated or you can install a higher powered battery and run wires to power a variety of equipment options. *Raymarine*, *Lowrance* and *Eagle Fish Finder* are some of the top names.

5. **Plumbing and hoses** can be installed for live bait tanks to circulate the water and keep bait alive.

6. **Mounts**: Individual or multi-use mounts and tracks, with or without extenders, can be installed on the kayak to hold all sorts of equipment including rods, electronics and cameras for 'catch, photo and release' anglers.

7. **Seats**: The molded seats in most kayaks are not very comfortable for the long haul so padded supportive seats and backrests can be added to the kayak.

8. **Bimini shade covers**: A small canopy on a frame keeps the sun off you or your equipment.

9. **Additional lashing, cleats, anchors and rigging systems** are also available and come as complete kits or DIY pieces in many different styles.

10. **Transportation devices**: From car racks to trailers, there are several ways to get your kayak to the water. Once there, portable, foldable carts can make the job of actually getting the kayak to the launch site much easier.

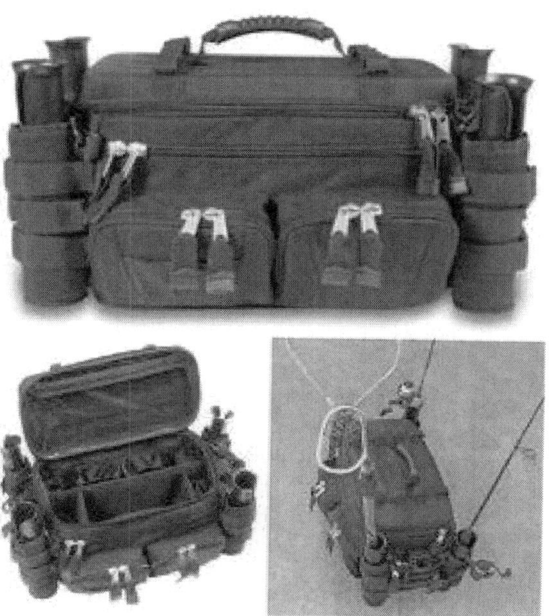

For more outfitting tips please visit:
*http://www.topkayaker.net/Articles/FishDive/AnglerKayaks.html*

# Carrying the Kayak and Gear

In order to get your kayak and gear to the water, you have to consider different options for transport. A kayak can be tied down to the roof of any car on foam or some other padding or set into a carrying rack. It is possible to carry one in the bed of a pickup truck with the tailgate down, but the length of a salt water fishing kayak may make that impractical. *Trailering* is always an option, but that is generally more expensive.

No matter how the kayak is transported, it is important to make sure all the gear is secure, either in the kayak or in the vehicle. Once you arrive at the launch site, there are several choices for actually getting into the water. With a wheeled cart, the kayak can be loaded in the parking lot and rolled to the edge of the water. Many carts are foldable so you don't have to worry about leaving one behind. This is particularly convenient if you plan to make stops during a longer trip.

For live bait and bringing fish home to eat, ice has to be included in coolers or lined wells. Special products are available for keeping things cold, but that will also depend on the length of your fishing trip.

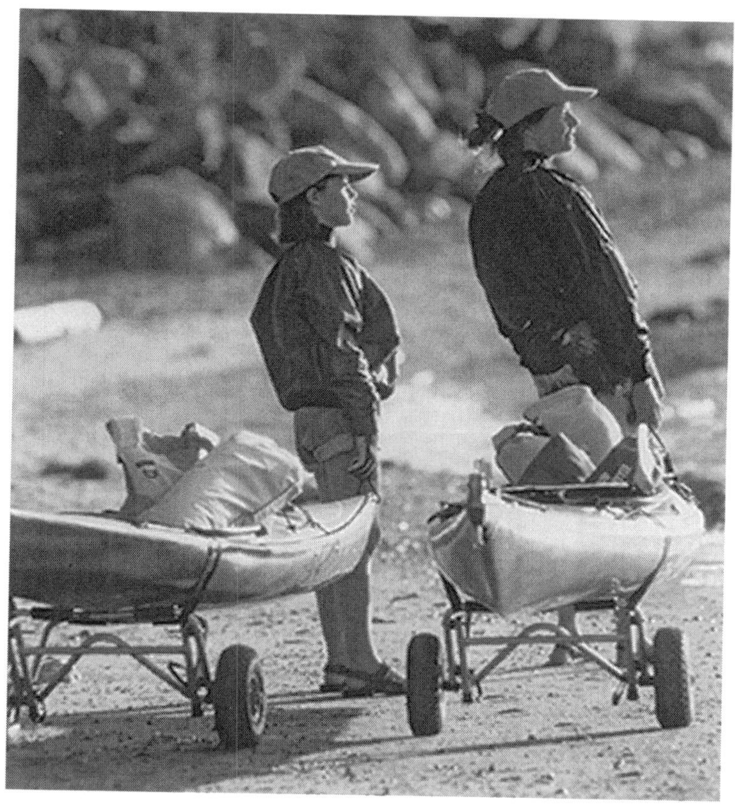

# Kayak Rigging and Anchors

In order to stay in one place and enjoy the fishing, an **anchor** or **stake out pole** is an easy to install and use accessory. The most efficient way to utilize these features is to install an anchor trolley system that runs from the bow to the stern of the kayak. The anchor is attached to a ring or karabiner on a continuous loop of line that can be tied off in any position. This allows the kayak to move with the wind to avoid turning broadside and capsizing. The trolley system has the advantage of allowing you to bring the anchor to the bow to pull up because this is where the greatest buoyancy is. There are plenty of kits available or you can buy the individual pieces because this is very easy to install as a DIY project.

The most common type of anchor used by kayak fishermen in ***rocky areas*** is the ***1.5 or 3 pound folding anchor***. When this anchor is deployed, the fins open up and grab onto the rocks or tree roots. The best way to avoid damage to the sea bottom is to paddle back to and past the anchor and then raise it up.

The ***2.2 lb. (1 kg) Bruce style anchor is best for sandy conditions*** or silt and mushroom anchors are also used on sand or mud but are heavier since they don't grip onto something. Brush grippers are excellent when you are fishing in marsh grass, cattails or brush and tree limbs.

A ***stake out pole*** is another way to anchor in a very shallow area like flats. Store-bought poles are great, but PVC tubing or even an old fishing rod can work just as well. The stake can either go through the ring on the trolley or a line attached to the stake can be clipped on. Clipping on the line provides better play if the tide is rising.

For very calm conditions in a minimal current, a ***drift chute*** that opens like a parachute may be enough to keep a kayak in place. This is also a good option for trolling. Another benefit of the chute is to add drag when fighting a big fish.

No matter what type of anchor is used, it is imperative to be aware of wave and wind conditions so the kayak is not swamped. ***Quick-release jam cleats*** are popular because the rope can be released easily in any conditions. A float on a line to the anchor allows you to locate the anchor later if you are forced to cut or release the line without being able to haul the anchor back on board. This works either with or without a pulley anchor lift system.

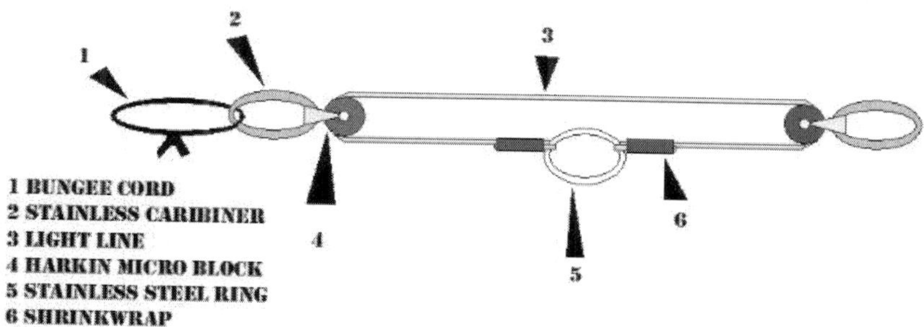

# CHAPTER 4 – SAFETY AND SELF-RESCUE

## Safety Equipment

Aside from having a safe kayak, PFD and paddle, a number of other pieces of safety equipment are available. Unfortunately, no one can buy common sense, but everyone can demonstrate an awareness of the weather and water conditions and be adequately prepared.

Boating regulations in most states, provinces and countries require basic items such as an approved PFD, a whistle or horn, something with which to bail out water and lights when out before dawn and after dusk. The regulations for any area where you want to paddle should be checked for other requirements such as licenses or permits, additional equipment and official sunrise and sunset times. Most PFDs have pockets, straps and loops for holding things like a whistle, knife, strobe light and other small gear.

***Additional safety equipment includes***:

- Paddle leash and spare paddle
- Compass (in all cases) and GPS device (if kayaking well off shore)
- Knife to quickly cut anchor lines or fishing line and ropes you might get tangled up in if you capsize
- Spray skirt to keep water out of the cockpit of an SIK in bad weather or rough conditions

- Bilge hand pump or scoop and a sponge
- Throw bag for rescue and tow rope
- Paddle floats for stability when re-entering a kayak
- Strobe light for an emergency or dark conditions
- Air horn for use at night, in fog or when near busy boating channels
- Basic first aid kit
- Emergency blanket
- VHF radio for contacting other marine craft and emergency personnel

Bringing this equipment on the kayak is one thing, but you should know how to use each item – through practice, not just by reading directions – before you set out. Stowing everything so nothing gets lost is also an important consideration. All kayaks have hatches opening to some type of storage compartment. These are a great place to store gear if they haven't been converted to bait or fish storage. Dry bags and other water-tight containers are available that can be placed in a hatch or strapped to the top deck. Deck bags that can be attached to the bow deck have storage space as well as pockets, hooks and straps. Milk crate style boxes are also a great way to hold gear and DIY rod holders and can be strapped behind the cockpit.

***Another, often overlooked safety issue is visibility.*** In this case, that means whether or not other boaters can see the kayak from a distance to avoid accidents. Color is a key factor in providing good visibility. Yellow and shades of bright orange are the most visible colors out on open water. Bright lime green and pink are not quite as easily seen but red, blue, green, black and white are almost invisible. In the event that the float plan takes you near heavily trafficked areas, a safety flag on a 4 foot pole can be installed at the stern. This is also effective for kayaking in mild swells.

# What to Do If You Capsize

The first thing that needs to be stated is that a PFD should always be worn when in a boat. Even strong swimmers can be pulled under water or become fatigued and drown without a life saving device. The possibility of capsizing is very real, so remaining calm and knowing what to do is vital. A sudden dip in cold water can be disorienting and affect your muscles so quickly you are unable to help yourself, so practicing how to capsize and recover is an important part of learning how to kayak.

Capsizing near shore in calm water usually leaves a paddler feeling silly. You should signal others that you have gone in the water and that you are all right. Gather any gear that has begun to float away, especially the paddle. If possible, right the kayak and tow it to shore with the end line either by walking or swimming with a modified side stroke. There is always the option for re-entry using self or assisted rescue techniques (discussed below), but be aware of any wetness and possible changes in the weather.

# What Not to Do When You Capsize

The most important advice for someone who has capsized is **do not panic**.

**Do not** let your equipment float away.

**Do not** stay in the water longer than necessary, especially if it is cool or the weather is bad.

Also, **do not attempt** to reenter the kayak if it is damaged or not stable. You could fall right back in!

# Self and Assisted Rescue Techniques

## Paddle Float

In open, relatively calm water, re-entry is possible without a paddle float, but using one makes it much simpler. **A paddle float is an inflatable or foam sleeve that fits over the blade of the paddle to keep that end afloat**. The other end can be secured in the rigging across the kayak just aft of the cockpit or held on to along the coming. With the paddle set as an outrigger on the up-righted kayak, pull your body up onto the deck, pivot so that you can put your legs into the cockpit one at a time while turning and holding the paddle float for support. Re-gain your correct center-line posture and empty the water out of the kayak. By remaining low over the boat, you keep the center of gravity low so it is less likely to tip again.

## Side by Side

For an assisted rescue, two kayaks should 'raft up' which means positioning them bow to stern and spanning both with a paddle. The seated kayaker holds the edge of the other cockpit to provide additional stability and the swimmer reenters the kayak the same way he would in an unassisted rescue. Get situated, make sure the paddle is at hand and pump out the water.

## X Rescue

A kayak over kayak rescue involves the rescuer pulling the overturned boat over his deck to drain it. The kayak is then turned over and returned to the water parallel to the rescue boat. The rescuer holds the other cockpit for stability. The swimmer pulls himself onto his kayak and is ready to go.

## T Rescue

If you have rolled and are still underwater, another boat can approach you at your seat where you will grab the bow and pull yourself up while performing a hip snap.

# Universal Communication

Five basic messages are recognized universally by paddlers to share information over the sounds of the water. These are similar in concept to those used by soldiers on a silent patrol.

- ***Stop*** – Hold the paddle with both hands straight up over your head. Other paddlers should stop safely as soon as they can and wait for additional signals.

- ***Help/ Emergency*** – The paddler can blow three long blasts on a whistle (which should be standard equipment attached to the life vest). With the paddle held up vertically, hand just above the lower blade, the paddler should wave the paddle side to side. Unless another paddler is specifically trained in emergency response, all paddlers should remain at a safe distance.

- ***All Clear*** – The paddle is held still with one hand, straight up in the air.

- ***Directions*** – Hold the paddle vertically, straight and high, in the direction to proceed. This should always be to the clear path, not towards an obstacle or hazard.

- ***Are you OK?*** – With the hands, point to the person in question and tap the top of your head three times.

# CHAPTER 5 – MOVING THE KAYAK

## Getting into the Kayak

The most basic way to get into a kayak is to place the bow into the water with the stern on the beach. You then sit on the back deck of the kayak, place your feet in the cockpit and carefully slide your legs into the boat until you are seated. With a little shifting side to side and a push with the paddle, you are afloat.

***If the beach is too rocky***, the bank is elevated or you don't want to risk damaging an expensive boat, the procedure will be slightly different. The kayak will be placed in the water parallel to the water's edge and one end of the paddle will rest on the shore while the other extends across the kayak behind the cockpit. With most of your weight on the paddle shaft and back rim of the cockpit, you will step into the boat one foot at a time in a crouch position, then extend your legs and assume the correct paddling position. When you are launching from a dock or elevated bank, you will also use this technique depending on the height of the dock relative to the kayak.

Most public launching areas are in protected inlets, but it is important to know how to deal with waves if you are touring along open coastline or small islands.

For any ***entry into active surf***, place the kayak close to the edge of the water with the bow just touching water when the wave rolls in.

Make sure all gear is secured and quickly get into the boat. Fasten the spray deck and be sure to hold on to the paddle.

Push yourself with your hands into the water keeping the kayak pointing directly into the wave line and begin paddling. If the boat gets pushed sideways back to shore, it will probably result in capsizing.

***Landing a kayak through the waves*** is a matter of timing similar to that of surfing. Instead of riding the front of a wave, however, you wait for the wave to pass under you, and then paddle to keep up with it. With an extra strong stroke, get on top of the wave at the very end for an extra boost onto the beach.

Get out quickly when you can't go any farther and don't forget the paddle! Hold on to the boat or line, too, so the next wave doesn't pull it back out.

No matter where you are entering a kayak, there are **several basic rules to always keep in mind**:

- Move carefully and smoothly, not abruptly
- Maintain three points of contact – two feet and one hand, two hands and one foot
- Keep your center of gravity as low as possible
- Hold on to the paddle
- Establish yourself in the kayak over the center line

# Correct Seating Position

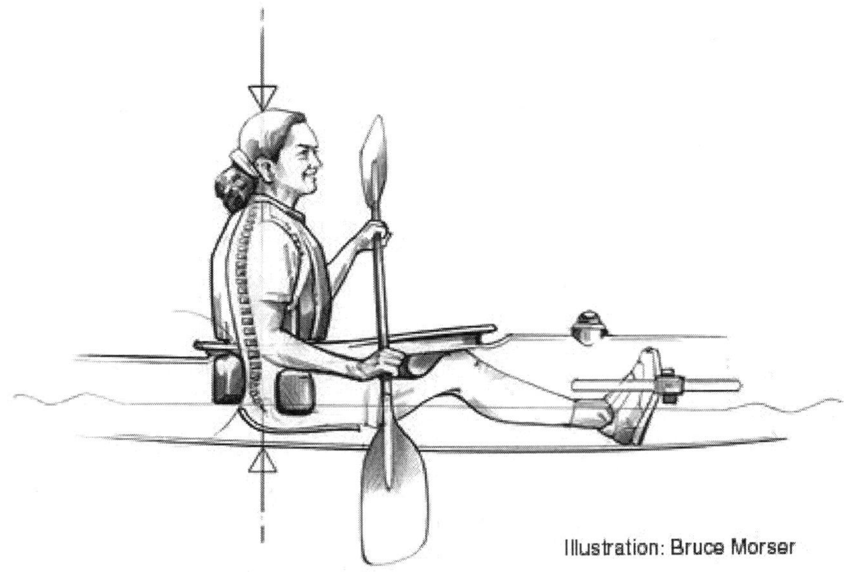

Illustration: Bruce Morser

Good posture is essential for effective paddling and minimizing the chances of back strain or even injury. This does not mean a forced upright posture, but rather sitting with your back straight, chin up, shoulders back comfortably and arms loose at your sides. You are neither slouching nor leaning back. Maintaining a strong, flexible core helps make this a natural position.

Most kayaks are equipped with a **back rest or a back strap**, but that is only meant for moderate support in the correct seating position. It is not designed to lean all your weight back on. Lounging back is just as potentially damaging as slouching. A variety of seats that provide better support and have comfortable padding are made for fishing kayaks so try out a few to see which suits you the best.

There are **adjustable foot rests** in kayaks that should be set so your feet rest against them and your knees are slightly bent and angled to the sides of the cockpit. In this position, there is less strain in your thighs and lower back, and your knees help to provide balance. SOT kayaks may have thigh straps to help hold you and provide resistance for leaning.

# Balance

Depending on overall length, beam (width) above and below the water and the shape of the hull, the buoyancy and stability of each kayak is different. There is a difference between ***initial stability***, which is a greater range of lean and stability while sitting still in the kayak and ***secondary stability*** that makes them less stable at entry or sitting still but more stable underway. This section will discuss balancing skills the paddler must learn and practice for successful maneuvering the kayak.

**To maintain balance in a kayak**, you have to remain loose, keep your upper body centered in the kayak and not overextended. If you stiffen up, you are working against the kayak instead of working as an extension of it. In calm water, it is good practice to experiment with different body movements in the kayak so you can develop a feel for the boat and the water. The differences between initial and secondary stability can be determined and you can decide which feels better to you. Most fishing kayaks are made with a wider beam for greater overall stability, but it is still a matter of personal preference.

**The way your body leans will exert different forces on the kayak** relative to the center of gravity. While it is usually best to keep your chin and spine in line with the center of the boat, various water conditions may require the paddler to lean a certain way to utilize current or the waves.

- ***The body lean*** means leaving your butt basically flat on the seat while you bend sideways from the waist. This does not affect the stability of the boat and is used for a sweep stroke or rudder stroke.

- ***The bell buoy lean*** is similar except that you shift your weight to one hip and maintain a straight spine - no bending at the waist. This position counteracts a pull to one side or keeps you upright in choppy or changing.

- ***The J-lean*** involves using your whole body to maintain balance while your hands are busy with fighting or landing a fish. You thrust your ribs to one side while lifting the opposite knee and hip. Your head remains over the center line. Bend your neck slightly toward the raised hip or away from the side of the lean.

These moves are the elements on which advanced skills are based. Learning and practicing them at the beginning assures you of a quick transition to white water.

# Basic Paddle Grip

The correct grip makes the process of paddling more efficient just like holding a baseball bat or golf club the right way improves performance. By learning that grip and using it every time you pick up the paddle the paddle becomes an extension of your arms and aids in control of the boat.

**The correct grip** involves grasping the shaft with both hands over your head and your elbows at right angles (90°) equal-distant to the blades. Your control, or dominant hand should have a straight wrist and the power (concave) side of the blade should be facing the water. Bring the paddle and yours arms straight down in front of you without loosening the control hand. The blade on the control side should now be vertical with the power side of the blade facing forward. Without using a death grip, the control hand should never loosen on the paddle – that is done solely by the opposite hand.

# The Wet Exit

If you have not perfected the Eskimo roll, the easiest and safest way to exit from a capsized kayak is to maintain a forward curl position with your chin tucked towards your chest. Then, perform a forward roll motion holding on to the kayak with one hand and drawing your legs smoothly out of the cockpit.

If you are wearing a spray deck, wait until you are oriented upside down, hold the paddle to your midsection, pull the handle to release the cover and draw your legs out. You should perfect this move first without using the spray deck, then practice with it.

With the aid of the PFD, you will easily come to the surface. Hopefully, you still have hold of your paddle and the kayak and can either head for shore, have another kayaker assist you or perform an unassisted rescue.

# Rolling

In the arctic, Inuit Indians learned how to roll their water craft as a way of avoiding getting out into the cold water after capsizing. When the move is done frequently enough, it becomes a continuous motion, the source of the name 'Roll'. There are different techniques to achieve this move but they are all based on the same general principles.

Grip the paddle in both hands alongside the kayak and lean to that side until you capsize.

Once you are completely turned over, raise your back arm (still gripping the paddle) out of the water onto the back of the kayak.

Sweep the front paddle in a large arc across the top of the water while arching your back to the rear deck.

While bending from the waist to continue bringing the kayak around, keep your head back along the deck until the kayak is righted, then sit up.

The same roll can be done with a brace motion instead of a sweep.

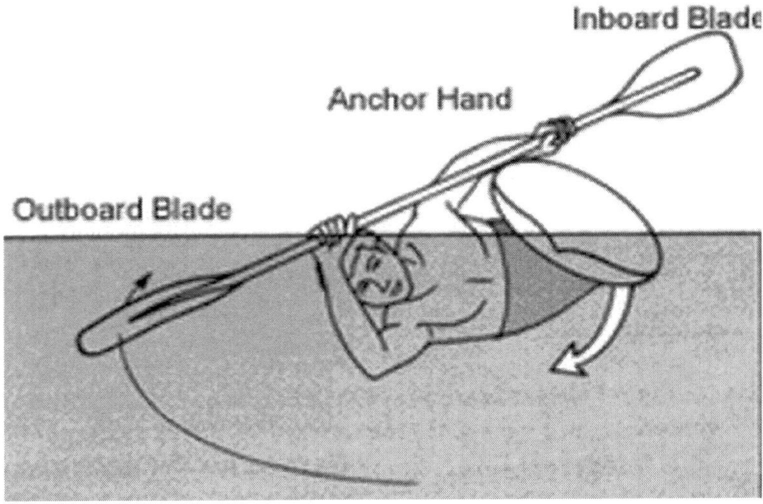

# Paddling

## Forward and Backward Strokes

**B**efore identifying specific strokes, ***several basic elements should always be kept in mind.***

It's all in the torso! The rotation of your torso and shoulders supplies the power and reach for each stroke.

Maintain control of the paddle! Keep a secure grip with the control hand and only allow rotation with the opposite hand to maintain the effectiveness of each stroke.

Don't drown the paddle! A silly statement, but it serves to point out that while the blade of the paddle should remain underwater during the power phase of the stroke, it should be as close to the surface as possible.

For a good **forward stroke**, you need to insert the blade cleanly into the water as close to the edge of the kayak as possible with the power side of the blade at a right angle to the direction of motion. Your lower arm should remain straight until the very end of the stroke.

Pull on the lower shaft as if it is staked into the ground and move the kayak forward.

Push against the upper part of the shaft with your upper are and keep that elbow below or just at shoulder level. As you go through the stroke, your arm will come across in front of your face.

With rotation of the torso, continue to bring the lower blade alongside the boat back to your hip. The upper hand will drop down and the lower elbow will begin to bend.

At this point, you will be simultaneously lifting the lower arm and extending the opposite arm forward and straight to be ready for the next stroke.

The **backward stroke** is basically the same thing in reverse. Do not change your grip on the shaft of the paddle. Rotate your torso as much as possible to place the blade as far back as possible.

With the paddle close to the edge of the boat, draw it forward through the water as you 'untwist' your torso.

When the blade reaches your feet, you will begin rotating to the opposite side to be ready to plant that blade in the water.

Remember to keep the water arm straight so you are truly transferring the power of your core to the paddle.

## Stopping

**S**imply ceasing to paddle will not stop a kayak. Stopping it requires you to **stick the blade into the water** right at your side with the blade **perpendicular to the kayak**. Try to hold the paddle straight until the resistance begins to turn the kayak. Quickly stick the paddle into the water at the other side and repeat the procedure until you have stopped.

## Forward and Reverse Sweep Strokes

The **forward sweep stroke** is the primary method of **turning the kayak**. It does not interfere with the steady rhythm of paddling but allows you to alter course without missing a beat.

To turn, you reach forward as far as possible and stick the blade into the water. Instead of drawing the paddle along the side of the kayak, you will reach out with a straight lower arm and pull the paddle back in an arc.

When the water blade draws back close to the stern of the kayak, the paddle should be flipped and raised from the water. Do not let the blade hit the side of the boat!

The kayak will continue to turn if the boat has remained stable and the blade comes out of the water cleanly.

**'Edging' the kayak** involves changing your balance slightly by lifting your knee on the up side of the paddle and shifting weight to the water blade side and helps make sweep strokes more effective.

The **reverse sweep stroke** is the opposite of the forward sweep and can be used to slow forward motion.

Without changing your grip on the paddle, place the blade into the water as far back as possible while rotating your torso and shoulders for the best extension. Draw the water blade forward in a wide arc.

When the forward and reverse sweep strokes are used together, the kayak will turn more quickly.

## Draw Stroke

This stroke is used to **move the kayak sideways**. Rotate your body to the side to which you want to move.

Extend the paddle out from the edge of the kayak while making sure the power face of the blade is facing the boat.

Lift your knee on the paddle side and draw the paddle in towards the boat.

As the paddle nears the side of the boat, use your wrists to change the angle of the blade 90° and without taking the blade out of the water, push the paddle out away from the boat to the position you started in. This is called an underwater recovery and is used to minimize the noise and splash of a regular paddle stroke.

Twist the blade so the power side faces the boat and repeat the moves until you reach your spot.

This stroke has to be done at a central point along the kayak to avoid turning.

## Stern Rudder

The stern rudder movement is used only for **slight adjustments to the direction of the kayak**. It is not intended to stop the boat or turn it – a forward sweep is the best way to do that.

Place the paddle alongside the stern with a straight lower arm with the drive face of the blade facing the kayak. Hold it in place until the course is corrected.

## Bracing

Low and high braces are **maneuvers used** to help a tipping kayaker **regain stability**. The paddle is used to provide just enough support to keep the kayak upright while the paddler uses leg and hip movements to stabilize the kayak.

The **low brace** is done by laying the paddle on top of the water with the drive face up. The paddle is kept low with both hands lower than the elbows. More support is provided if the blade is farther away from the kayak. The paddler's weight is temporarily supported by this brace to provide time for him to stabilize the boat. For additional support while sitting still, the paddle float can be attached.

The **high brace** involves holding the paddle under the surface of the water with the drive face down. The hands should be above the elbows and not extended forward. This brace is more powerful than the low brace and is really only used in sea kayaking if you are surfing the waves.

These moves should be practiced and mastered, however, because they are important elements used in rolling!

For an excellent animated tutorial for beginning skills please visit:
kayakpaddling.net

# Understanding the Wind, Waves and Tides

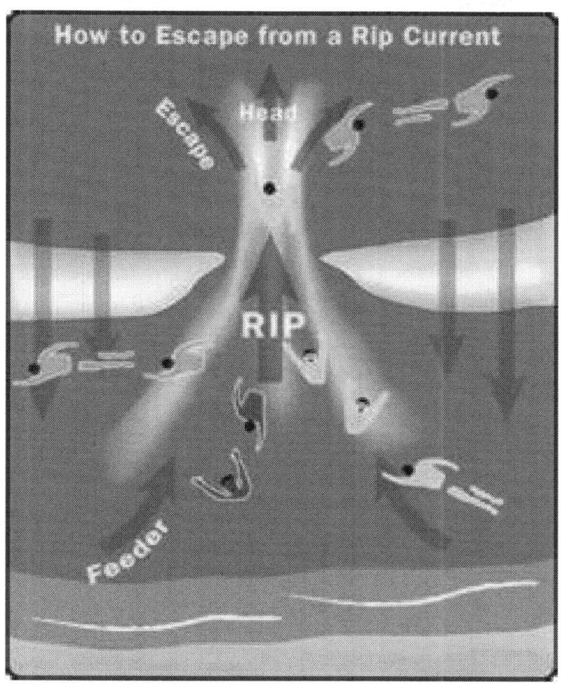


**O**ut on the ocean or even in bays and estuaries, the tide and winds can be dangerous to a beginning kayaker. Ebb and rip tides prevent you from returning to the shore easily and the wind not only pushes you off course but also raises the height of the waves. Other conditions create troughs that seem to trap the kayak. Navigation charts and tables can provide you with basic information about the area to help plan the safest route, but not all water movements are accounted for on paper.

To learn how to handle these conditions, going out with a guide or another highly experienced paddler is the wise thing to do.

The ***Beaufort Wind scale*** rates the force of the wind into 12 categories. A beginning paddler should not go out in wind over level 2 or 3. Level 2 breezes are measured at 4 – 7 mph or 7 – 11 km/h. Level 3 is 8 – 12 mph and 12 – 19 km/h. Whitecaps can form at level 4 but most commonly at level 5. A level 6 wind blowing over the ocean for two days can create waves up to 18′ or 5.5 meters high. Level 7 is considered near-gale force and level 12 is the minimum wind speed for a storm to be classed as a hurricane.

**Chop** is one type of offshore waves and is created by brief winds blowing over a small area to create random waves. In this situation, remain calm and loose and continue to paddle through it. These waves cause a bumpy ride but don't exert much influence on the kayak.

**Swells**, the other type of offshore waves, are the large rolling waves created by wind blowing in the same direction over great distances of the ocean. As they approach the shore the direction and strength of the wind affects them in different ways. An offshore wind (from land to the ocean) causes the waves to become steeper and break in a crash. Lee or following winds press down on the tops of the waves so the water dances along the top of the wave.

With other conditions affecting the characteristics of offshore sea water such as tides or the mouths of bays and rivers, it is important to learn about these conditions before setting out on a trip.

A tremendous amount of data for other water characteristics or what is called structure such as eddies, shallows, flats, gullies, humps, boulders, stony outcroppings, ridges and trenches is also available. Scouting an area at low tide is also a good way to find these features and sandbars. Underwater wrecks are also a great place to find fish and are frequently noted on charts. Good navigation skills including reading a compass or following GPS are a needed to not only find these special places but to return to port. In addition to studying the charts, it is always a great practice to talk to local fishermen and outfitters to learn more about different spots and how the fish move.

# Navigation and Buoys

The concept of navigation includes the equipment to help you find your way and the knowledge to use it correctly. A **compass and map** should be enough for most trips as long as you plan to follow the coast or shoreline. For crossing a more open stretch of water where the use of visible landmarks is limited, a compass and chart along with prior examination of the area are required. A GPS system is the most reliable way to know where you are and where you need to go. It is always a good idea to talk to someone locally who can share information about the waters you plan to paddle.

**Navigation charts** show land, the main channels in the waterways and tide and navigational marker information. The color red is always associated with a pointed marker and green is rectangular. The simple way to know which way to go through them is the phrase 'red, right, returning' which is universally meant as keeping the red markers on your right side as you are returning to port. Other specialty markers are used in crowded waterways, intersections or around sunken or natural obstacles.

Taking a class offered by maritime organizations is the best way to understand navigation as well as basic seamanship.

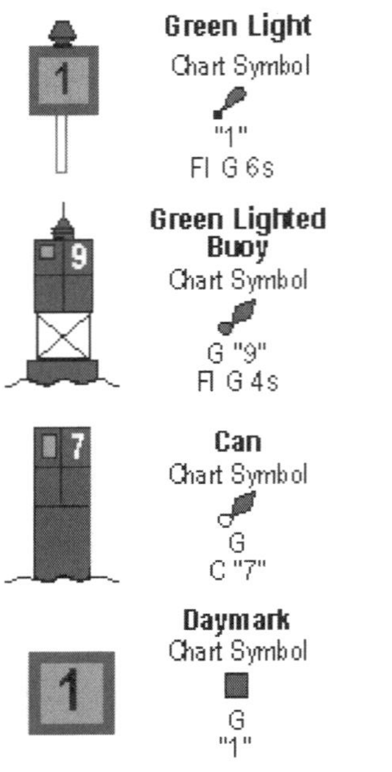
Port Side Lateral System
As seen entering from seaward
(Green Light Only
Odd Numbered Aids)
Green Light
Chart Symbol
"1"
Fl G 6s
Green Lighted Buoy
Chart Symbol
G "9"
Fl G 4s
Can
Chart Symbol
G
C "7"
Daymark
Chart Symbol
G
"1"

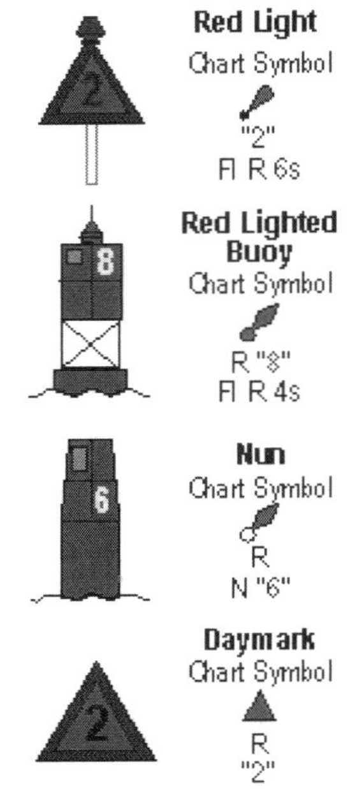
Starboard Lateral System
As seen entering from seaward
(Red Light Only
Even Numbered Aids)
Red Light
Chart Symbol
"2"
Fl R 6s
Red Lighted Buoy
Chart Symbol
R "8"
Fl R 4s
Nun
Chart Symbol
R
N "6"
Daymark
Chart Symbol
R
"2"

# CHAPTER 6 – FISHING STYLES

## Ways to Choose

Everything comes full circle when you are trying to match your gear to your style of fishing since there are several different ways to decide how you want to fish and they, in turn, affect the choice of kayak and gear. Many kayak fishermen don't take any chances and prepare for several alternatives and buy different equipment to use at different times. All this depends on your commitment to salt water kayak fishing and how much money you want to spend.

Many anglers are on the hunt for specific species of fish, others choose based on seasonal movements of fish, still others decide based on whether or not they want to anchor, drift or be underway and yet others like particular spots for fishing. Since these choices are inter-related and more pertinent to the fishing part of the equation, the discussion of salt water kayak fishing styles will be based on the movement of the kayak.

## At Anchor

This works several ways in that you can fish the flats, marshes or open water. In the flats or other slim water, using an anchor or stake pole **allows you to fish where the bottom or shore conditions make it impossible to wade**. *Jigging* and *fly casting* are the best techniques for the most part, but in rocky conditions where there are abrupt obstacles and holes, dropping a line also provides the possibility of catching a larger offshore fish that has come in to feed. You can actually fish the top and midsection of the water column.

Anchoring offshore lets you take advantage of two separate opportunities – *casting* and *jigging* into deeper water or towards shore for troughs and shallows and bottom fishing. Larger fish tend to congregate next to a ledge or the upper edge of a channel near the flats for feeding. Spot fishing, or standing and looking for fish activity is also popular at anchor.

In any case, fishing from a kayak in these areas has the advantage of the line being able to reach spots that are impossible to access from other boats. Not only that, but a kayak does not cast much of a shadow and can be propelled gently enough to not create much silting or other disturbances. The key thing to be careful of, however, is the changing tide – you do not want to get caught on the flat or up a creek bed when the water level drops. That is why tide charts and information from local marine shops are so important.

In deep water where you want to catch the fish that feed on the bottom, dropping a line so the bait lies on the seabed is easy. When the tide turns, however, adding a weight ahead of the bait will keep the line from rising in the current, lifting the bait off the bottom. Jigging with a quick-drop lure can work the whole water column and is good for deep bottoms and wrecks.

## Drifting

This technique, drifting, and poling, which means **pushing the kayak along by pushing against the bottom**, is another successful way to fish the flats and open water.

*Jigging, bottom fishing* or *free lining* will catch different fish depending on the depths to which you allow your live or artificial bait or lure to go. To avoid paddling or poling altogether and for the opportunity to stand and sight fish, start at an up current or upwind section of the flat and follow the natural flow of the water. With such shallow water, flats are not usually subject to any waves, so gentle, steady movements keep you secure in the kayak.

Drifting can also be accomplished in deeper water on a very calm day or with a drift chute. Unlike an anchor that is designed to stop a boat, the open chute will create enough drag to significantly slow down a kayak in a current or strong breeze. Buoying the chute to drag closer to the surface will not interfere with a line working on or near the bottom.

An ancient method of fishing has a new interest among kayak fishermen – net casting for bait and other small fish and even shrimp! Even from a sitting position, a net can be cast from the kayak and the catch dumped into a bucket. It takes some practice and a good command of balancing the kayak by knee, leg and hip positions.

With these choices for slow movement and relatively flat water, the mid and top levels of the water column are reachable as well as the surface.

## Underway

**Fishing while moving**, whether by paddle or peddle, **is called *trolling*.** Since fish, even the largest, come to the surface to feed, the lure or bait does not have to trail the kayak at much of a depth – several feet (one meter) down is enough. In warmer weather, the fish stay further down, so adding a trolling sinker or using wire line to add weight may be a good idea. The lure or bait should trail the kayak at roughly 50′ to 100′ (15m to 30m).

When a fish takes the bait, the kayaker must react quickly and begin the process of hooking the fish and reeling him in. This is the definitely the time to have a tether or leash on the rod in case the fish takes you completely by surprise! This is where the real test of the fisherman begins – fighting the big one to land him!

The speed at which the kayak travels impacts the kinds of fish that are likely to take the bait. Inshore, bass and mackerel are attracted at 2 to 4 knots and open ocean fish like tuna, mahi mahi or kingfish respond to lures moving at 5 to 8 knots. Even larger, deeper dwelling big game fish need a tremendous effort of over 10 knots to become interested! This is possible, but be ready for the ride and fight of your life.

# A Word About Fly Fishing

**K**ayak fishing has enjoyed a tremendous surge in popularity recently and part of that is due to the ability to engage in **fly fishing**. The kayak enables the angler to cover large distances without excessive exertion.

Fly fishermen have discovered the advantage of stealth when using a kayak. The paddler can quickly move to a spot with fish activity, put down the paddle and cast. A shorter than usual rod is best because of the limited range of motion for casting in a kayak, but techniques can easily be developed to maximize leverage to attain distance. One thing to take note of, though, is whether the rod is long enough to clear the bow of the kayak while bringing in a fish – you don't want it to swim under the kayak and wrap up the line! The shallow draft of the kayak also allows the fisherman to get into skinnier water as well.

***One issue particular to fly fishing is the use of a stripping bucket for loose line.*** Since there is not much distance from your hands to the bottom of the kayak and not usually much effect from wind, simply letting it coil on the deck between your legs works fine for many fishermen. It is a matter of preference, but without a bucket or something to collect the line, the deck must be clear of other lines and equipment. If there is a spray skirt, even if it is not completely attached, the front section provides a spot for the line to coil up on without being interfered with by other equipment.

While paddling to a particular spot, many anglers troll a line or two just to see what happens. This can also be done while fly fishing, but don't forget to secure the rod! Some fishermen set the rods into rod holders and others secure them under one leg and the opposite arm. Whichever method you choose, **don't forget to attach a tether or leash to the rod** in case you find the big one and it tries to take off with the equipment!

Unless you are at anchor, the wind and current will carry the kayak. In an onshore breeze, start out farther from shore so that you can cast straight in ahead of yourself as the boat moves in. As that distance is cut down, cast farther to the bow or stern until your casts are in a direct parallel line with the boat and paddle back out again. This can be tricky with waves, but as long as you move off before you are in the surf, things should go smoothly.

**In a tide situation**, you have to be aware that you are moving with the fly so it is more likely to sink than drag. That requires a little adjustment to get used to, but think of it like casting in a river. During the slack tide, cast like you would on a lake, keeping the bait or lure in the upper area of the water column. Large fish can be anywhere, but since they tend to stay in deeper water, you are not as likely to catch a real big one with this type of fly fishing.

**Fly fishing from a kayak in the open ocean** or bay requires certain precautions. Knowledge of the tides, winds and abruptly changing weather conditions is a must, and don't forget the possibility of being towed behind a monster fish. A kayak is much more susceptible to changes than larger boats are and control is necessary.

Once you have chosen a promising spot you can either drift or anchor and enjoy a special kind of fishing.

# The Finer Points of Gear

## Rods

Any kayak can be used to go fishing – even the plainest one right off the shelf. The amount of gear discussed in Chapter 3, however, points out that certain things are really necessary. That goes for fly fishing as well when you consider extras like rod holders, a net, an extra rod or two and maybe a line bucket. There are several differences, though between regular fly casting rods and those you would use on a kayak. **The general rule is lighter and shorter** as long as you still have a strong, flexible rod that can reach past the ends of the kayak.

For fishing rods in general, ***certain characteristics make some rods a better choice over others***. Any salt water fishing equipment should be approved for use in that environment and carefully cleaned off with fresh water after every outing, even if a particular piece wasn't used.

- **Closed face reels** have the advantage of being smaller and less likely to present maintenance issues. That cuts down on lost time on the water and the need to carry extra parts and tools.

- **Small spinning rods** are also relatively low maintenance and easy to store. They can be used with just one hand so the other can be used to maneuver the kayak.

- **Casting rods with small reels** are another easy to use choice for potentially larger fish.

- **Fiberglass rods** are more durable and generally less expensive than graphite rods. This is a good feature for gear that may get tossed around in the kayak or in transit or get lost overboard.

- **Stainless steel, brass or titanium rods** are particularly heavy duty.

- **Graphite rods** are the easiest with which to detect smaller, more tentative fish bites.

- Look for **rods that provide accurate casting and a comfortable feel.**

- **Two piece rods** and those that telescope are obviously convenient since they are easy to store.

- Top manufacturers include: *Abu Garcia, Berkley, Daiwa, Penn, Shakespeare* and *Zebco.*

## Hooks

Next to the rod and reel, the hook is one of the most important pieces of your gear. There are so many types of hooks for virtually every different type of fish, bait and water condition, but the important thing to consider is what you want to do with the fish once it is caught.

In any case, whether you are keeping the fish or releasing it, the hook needs to have a sharp point. The bard can be removed for the ability to release the fish most humanely and plain carbon hooks will corrode in salt water if they cannot be removed from the fish. Stainless steel will not corrode, so it will stay with the fish after its release if it cannot be taken out.

## Lines and Leaders

The lines and leaders that hold the hook are also of extreme importance. As a fisherman, that information should already be in your knowledge base, but aspects to consider are the strength of the line, its ability to float, sink, stretch and the size to diameter ratio for loading a reel. As a general rule, ***braided lines are strong but have no give so they are hard on the arms and shoulders during a prolonged fight.*** They are also so thin that they can cut through skin very easily so gloves are a must! The advantage of braided line, besides strength, is the lack of stretch which allows for better control of the bait or lure and easier detection of bites. It is also good in marshes and tall grasses since it cuts right through them.

**Monofilament and fluorocarbon lines** have their advantages and disadvantages as well, but a key point to check is the ability of any line to stay tied. Some hold knots better than or at least differently than others so double check your connections so the big one does not get away.

## Weights, Sinkers and Swivels

These are used to add distance to a cast and to bring or hold bait to certain depths. Aerodynamic shapes are the best for longer casts. Consider wired leads to add weight to a line for certain circumstances such as up tide ledgering and dropping a line into turbulent water. Swivels are not always necessary, but are the best way to reduce line twist, and snap swivels make switching lures much easier which is a big advantage to a kayak fisherman. Some anglers feel that the swivel is an unnecessary weight or that it may spook the fish while others feel they help attract the fish. Like everything else, with experience, it becomes a matter of choice.

## Lures

While lures tend to be a very personal issue for most fishermen, there are general considerations for all types. The size and similarity of your lure to the baitfish your target is likely to feed on is the key. Excellent construction is also a must so the lure doesn't come apart with a tentative nibble. Having the right size hook attached in the right place is the only way to hook the fish that your lure attracts. Some lures have bright markings, such as eyes, to entice its prey and creating a life-like movement by jigging or other techniques completes the picture.

To find out more about attaching hooks and lures tor your line please visit the following link: www.go-saltwater-fishing.com/tying-fishing-hooks.html

## Cutting Equipment

**E**quipment to cut line and bait as well as fouled rigging is important. A nail clipper attached to the PFD is a great way to cut line without the danger of being cut by a knife, and a knife and cutting board to fillet bait is also a good idea along with a general purpose fishing knife.

### *The Bottom Line*

Pardon the pun, but buying gear because of price is not the way to go. Something very expensive is not necessarily the best product and buying cheap things costs more in the long run due to the more frequent need to replace things. You can be economical and still get excellent gear.

# Where, When and What

Where to fish is more of a personal choice than an exact science. There are general recommendations, though, for locations, times of day and types of bait.

**Anywhere the surface is choppy** is a good place to look for fish.

Fish congregate around wrecks, reefs, rocky bottoms and beds of sea weeds or grasses.

**Early morning is a good time** to find large fish feeding closer to the surface.

**In warm weather, fish look for shade** under bridges, outcroppings and piers or they head deeper. They also need to eat more, so don't skimp on the bait!

**For deep water fishing**, shiny lures that move attract fish as do larger pieces of bait including live baitfish, mullet, shrimp and squid.

**For surf fishing**, fish are attracted by smell and vibration since sight is limited in the turbulence.

# Mothershipping

No, this is not a typo but a relatively new concept for deep sea fishing from kayaks. This is essentially a charter trip where a regular fishing boat with captain and possible crew take the kayakers out to sea. When they reach a promising spot, the kayaks are launched from the boat for fishing. Doing this saves time and energy while allowing the kayak fisherman the opportunity to go several miles or more out into open waters. The boat is available for assistance and as a place to store gear so the kayak does not need to be loaded with options for rods, hooks, baits, lures and the trophy fish you want to bring home.

# CHAPTER 7 – FIGHTING AND LANDING A BIG FISH

## Be Prepared

**A** screaming reel and a Nantucket sleigh ride are a tremendous rush, but you better be prepared! Catching big game fish is certainly exciting, but it requires a tremendous amount of preparation. You need to be physically fit to endure the workout of reeling in a large, fighting fish for an extended period of time. Upper body and arm strength as well as cardio vascular fitness are taxed to extremes while bringing home the largest of the trophy fish.

As a beginner, the best way to get started hunting for the big game fish is to hire a licensed kayak fishing guide. If that is not an option, you should at least talk to other kayakers who have landed the big ones and get some tips so you know what to expect. ***Wearing a PFD and knowing how to re-enter your kayak are key issues***, and you should have safety equipment available that you know how to use correctly! A compass, GPS and VHF radio are necessities on open water trips. A buddy or two can never hurt so at least there is someone to take pictures or help out if necessary.

Preparation also includes ***knowledge about the inclinations of these fish when they are hooked***. Some run, some go to the bottom and some even attack! Knowing what to do in each case means the difference between success and failure and maybe even safety and severe injury. Doing your research and making a plan are critical to the success of deep sea kayak fishing. You need to understand how the water and weather conditions affect the likelihood of running into different types of fish. Even more importantly, you need to seriously understand and accept your own ability. Overestimating your knowledge and skills can put you into a situation that puts you and others with you in danger.

Without adequate preparation, **it is sometimes better to let a big one get away**!

# Equipment

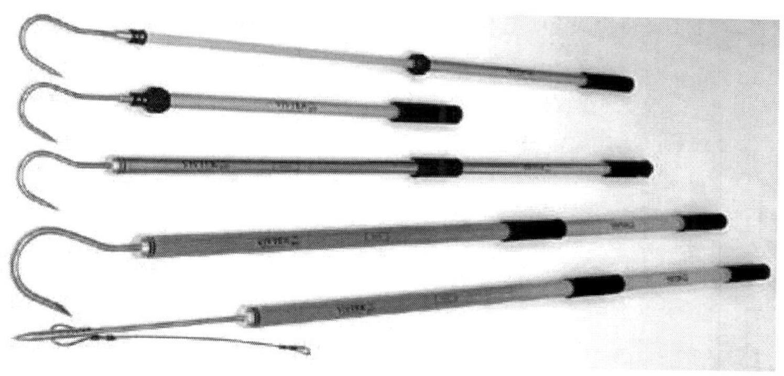

Interestingly enough, for the biggest fish, ***you want to keep your equipment to a minimum***. A small tackle box, portable fish finder, two rods and a net, gaff, club and safety knife are all you need. With more equipment on deck, you run the risk of having things in your way that may hurt you or get lost or damaged. A bait tank and unused items should be stowed behind the cockpit. Attaching a tether or leash to the gear that you will use is the best way to hold on to everything and flush mount rod pockets help hold the rod.

**The kayak** itself **should be wide enough** to remain stable – a beam of at least 28 inches. With many models to choose from, getting advice from an expert or other successful deep sea kayak fishermen is the best way to start. New kayaks are designed to maximize performance in terms of stability and speed, but overall safety is still the most important consideration.

Rods, lines and other technical pieces of equipment are chosen based on very personal preferences. The most common advice to beginners is to make the fight as quick as possible. This may be a little harder on you, but it is more humane to the fish and may ultimately be safer for you as well. To have that kind of control, kayak fishermen tend to prefer shorter rods for increased leverage. Be careful of the trade-off of clearing the bow while fighting a fish. Lighter drag on the line also seems to work more efficiently for kayak fishermen because too much drag is harder to respond to. The boat is more likely to be pulled over or the line may snap. It's easier to increase drag than it is to re-enter the kayak or re-string the line. Another way to increase drag during a long fight is to use a drift chute or to sit 'side saddle' with your feet over the edge dangling in the water. Just make sure to be back on or in the kayak before your catch gets too close!

When the struggle is almost at an end, some fish surprise you with a last burst of energy and frenzy. All types of fish have certain characteristics regarding their attempts to get away, so this is where preparation is so important. The ability to use your body to counteract the weight of the fish is unique to kayak fishing. Unlike fishing from a boat where you may be strapped in and have a harness, in kayak fishing you have to depend solely on your strength and skills. And in spite of some regular expectations, you always have to be prepared for the one that still tries to get away! With big game fish, it can be a matter of life and death if you are not ready for the strength and surprises these fish possess.

With knowledge and some experience, you will be able to outfit your kayak to your own personal liking. Keeping the gear you need closer to your dominant hand prevents you from having to cross over your body to reach for something. The opposite side is where you can install paddle hooks and electronic devices. Smaller tools such as pliers, safety knives and others can usually be attached to the PFD. Some companies have developed retractable tools so they can't get lost or in the way!

Always remember: **no fish is worth your safety or your life**! If it seems like you're in over your head, cut the line!

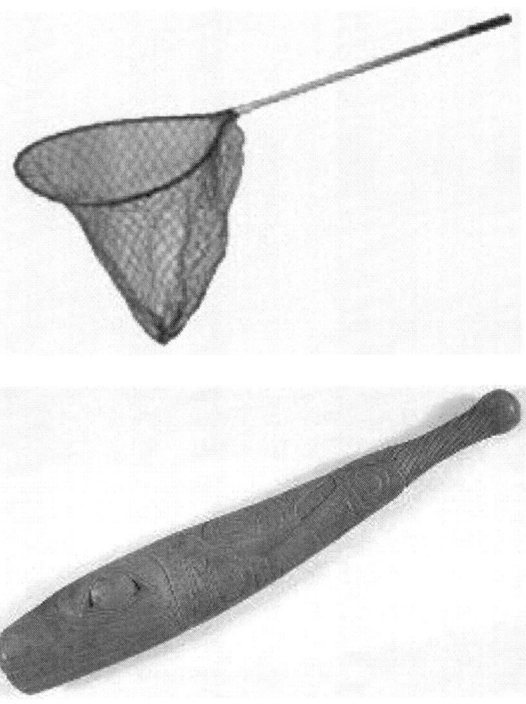

**A fishing club** is also called a 'priest' or a cosh. It can be made from metal, wood or bone and some are quite beautifully carved. Its purpose is to quickly kill a fish that may be too lively to safely bring on board.

# Catch and Release

**M**ore commonly now than in the past, most fishermen are likely to release the fish they catch, usually after photographing the results of their struggle. Shortening the fight is more humane to the fish so heavier tackle and circle hooks or J-hooks with crushed barbs are used as well as side saddle seating for the initial run. When handling a fish you intend to release, wear gloves or wet your hands to preserve the slime that covers fish to protect it from infection. Using a lip gripper and hook remover makes it easier to hold the fish and take care of the hook. Along these same lines, the body of the fish needs support when it is held out of the water, and the air needs to be removed with a venting tool from the air bladder of the deepest dwelling fish.

This is the most eco-friendly way to fish so that there are always plenty left for the next generation of fishermen. Take note, however, that holding a thrashing fish next to the kayak, dragging live bait or a string of caught fish may attract other predators that may want to steal the results of your hard work! Handle the fish quickly for release and stow any live fish in or on your kayak.

Another ecology tip is to be very careful with discarded line. Do not let coils of line loose in the water because any number of sea animals and birds may become tangled up. Carefully wrap up the line, cut through the circle and discard the lengths of string in a bag or your tackle box.

# CHAPTER 8 – PREPARING FOR A TRIP

## Getting the Idea

**A**s a beginner to the sport of kayak fishing, the best way to get involved is with a professional guide, an organized fishing group or competent friends who have experience on the water. If you are accustomed to fishing from a motor boat or large charter boat, the main difference to focus on is limiting the gear you will bring on the kayak.

A few short excursions to get the feel of the boat and how to balance it are important before you head out from shore very far or for an all day trip. You need to make note of different conditions you encounter in terms of tides, currents, winds and sun exposure and the amount of water you need to consume. It is not as easy as reaching into a cooler on the deck next to your captain's chair!

An excellent way to document these things is to rig up a video camera and talk to it as the day goes on. You can mention where you are, the weather and temperature, the type of rod, line and bait or lure you are using and anything else you observe in the process of casting, reeling in and landing different fish. This provides you with a digital record of the trip that can be referred back to at a later time and even compared to a similar trip in a different season or with different equipment.

# Planning a Short Trip

Among friends or strangers, planning for a trip requires complete honesty about ability and the willingness to work together. With a hired guide, there is no question as to who is responsible, but each person still needs to be responsible for himself.

In addition to personal experience, talking with others who have experience in that area as beneficial as guidebooks and local maps. Before heading out, the concept of **working as a group** needs to be clarified. This includes co-responsibility for maintaining communication, watching for sharks and weather changes and practicing personal safety and responsibility. **Roles for other specific functions are** then **assigned**. These roles include:

- ***Trip leader***: This person has overall responsibility for the group, preparations and knowledge of the proposed route and fishing locations. The leader essentially calls the shots – carries the map, compass, safety and rescue gear, repair kit and extra paddle. This person should be informed of medical or physical limitations of any group member and assign a second-in-command to provide back up or help. Awareness of the weather and being able to read the signs are also important.

- ***Sweep***: He should have strong paddling skills and be experienced in performing rescues. This paddler also keeps an eye on the whole group.

- ***Rescue***: All paddlers should understand that the two kayaks closest to someone in trouble are the initial responders if they are experienced in rescue techniques.

Everyone is responsible for carrying their own necessary gear and any extra can be divided up among group members.

When planning an inshore trip, the dock or marina can be a staging center for changing out gear or meeting for lunch to cut down on what is carried on the kayak. Don't ever cut down on the amount of drinking water you have available! It is crucial to maintain your body's hydration to prevent fatigue, dizziness or even confusion.

# Planning an Extended Trip

All the same guidelines apply for an extended trip as a short trip. For longer excursions, the need for extra food, water and possibly camping gear needs careful consideration. There is also a higher level of endurance required for long trips, so physical conditions or limitations need to be seriously assessed and accounted for.

There should be **designated contact persons** in the event that information needs to get 'home'. This person or people should also have a 'float plan' indicating fishing spots and the direction of travel should also be left with someone on land to keep track of the progress of the trip. The main contact person should also keep informed about the weather in the area where the group is expected to be so that delays don't cause a premature call for rescue. As part of the float plan, this person should have a brief biography of the group members including names, ages and general physical condition. There should also be a list of the equipment that is being used, especially in terms of safety and rescue, and information about any special skills someone in the group may have such as medical knowledge, or special needs such as a diabetic. In the event of staging a rescue, this knowledge can help the emergency responders be prepared. Although this may seem excessive and may never have to be used, it is vital if and when the situation does come up.

*Mothershipping* (discussed in Chapter 6) is a relatively new way to take part in an extended trip without the need of long-term planning. The ship is your floating home base for food, lodging and emergency assistance.

# Professional Guides

With the explosion in popularity of kayak fishing, many outfitters, professional guides and travel specialists run all types of trips. One tremendous advantage of this is having someone with experience in that particular locale along for the best tips and information. Another plus is that accommodations are probably included in the package. As a responsible traveler, however, it is important that you do a little research about the group or company to make sure they are, in fact, licensed professionals and have a good reputation.

paddling.com/paddle - site provides links to mothership tours, international trips, lodge based trips and other special interest activities.

# CONCLUSION

As an avid fisherman, you are now ready to find an outfitter so you can rent a kayak and hire a guide for a day to get started on the most exciting fishing you have ever experienced! With the information provided in this book, you have a good basis for having a successful and enjoyable experience salt water fishing from a kayak.

- You are now prepared to achieve the physical fitness needed for the extra demands of reeling in the big ones.
- You can make an intelligent choice of kayak, paddle, PFD, and clothing.
- You have a good idea of the add-ons available for rigging a fishing kayak.
- You understand the rationale for choosing certain fishing gear over other types.
- You appreciate the extra precautions necessary for safety.
- You have a basic understanding of the techniques used to balance, propel and self-rescue in a kayak.
- You have an introduction to the science of reading the tides, waves and winds.
- You can identify navigational markers and understand the position of a kayaker among other larger power boats.
- You understand the different types of fishing that can be done

from a kayak and the techniques to be successful.

- You appreciate the beauty and excitement as well as the danger of catching and bringing in the big one.

- You have learned how to plan and prepare for different types of trips and understand the use of a float plan and personal information left with a contact person at home.

- You have handy resources for finding additional information for each of these topics in the course of the text as well as other specific information in the Appendices section.

Join the millions of people around the world who have already experienced the freedom and true man versus nature feeling you can only find in a kayak! Once you do, you may never go back to using any other type of boat for salt water fishing. With this ages old, natural approach to fishing, you may develop a strong desire to practice conservancy and ecological preservation and help to ensure a clean, well-stocked fishing environment for generations to come.

Happy fishing!

*Please remember: This information is designed as an introduction and general guide to salt water kayak fishing. It does not replace the benefits obtained from taking kayaking lessons and the services of a licensed, professional guide.*

# APPENDICES

## Definitions and Classifications of Coastal Waters

*Open waters include:*

- **Coastal offshore** - all waters greater than two nautical miles from the coast. Heading offshore is a serious undertaking and operators must ensure they are properly prepared. Additional safety equipment ensures that operators have a means of raising the alarm in the event of an emergency. This equipment will provide an increased level of safety for all vessels heading offshore.

- **Coastal inshore** - all waters along the coast within two nautical miles.

*Inland waters include:*

- **Enclosed waters** - bays, inlets, estuaries and waterways that open to the sea.

- **Inland waters** - rivers, lakes and waterways that do not open to the sea.

**Water Class Definitions** as listed by the Sea Kayak Guides Alliance of BC (British Columbia)

**Class I**: Non-challenging protected waters with limited wind effect, little or no current, easy landings and ready access to land-based assistance.

**Class II**: Lightly populated areas with short crossings, moderate potential wind effects, gentle to moderate non-turbulent currents, easy to moderate landings and light surf beaches.

**Class III**: Exposed water, sparsely populated areas with more committing crossings, moderate to strong currents with turbulence, moderate to strong wind effects, ocean swells, difficult landings, surf beaches.

**Class IV**: Long committing crossings, uninhabited, rugged and exposed coast, strong turbulent currents, strong wind effects, large swells, difficult landings, exposed surf beaches.

# Environment and Etiquette

Since most recreational paddling (as opposed to competitive paddling) occurs in natural conditions, it is the responsibility of every paddler to follow the 'Leave no Trace' doctrine to preserve the beauty, safety and health of the environment. The bulk of the mission statement of the Sierra Club sums it up very well:

***Mission Statement:***

To explore, enjoy, and protect the wild places of the earth;

To practice and promote the responsible use of the earth's ecosystems and resources;

To educate and enlist humanity to protect and restore the quality of the natural and human environment; and to use all lawful means to carry out these objectives.

Following the philosophy of leaving no trace means more, however, than not littering. It is a conscientious effort to leave the land and water as undisturbed as possible. The Leave No Trace Center for Outdoor Ethics has seven basic principles to achieve that goal:

**Plan Ahead and Prepare**

- Know the regulations and special concerns for the area you'll visit.
- Prepare for extreme weather, hazards, and emergencies.
- Schedule your trip to avoid times of high use.
- Visit in small groups when possible. Consider splitting larger groups into smaller groups.
- Repackage food to minimize waste.
- Use a map and compass to eliminate the use of marking paint, rock cairns or flagging.

## Travel and Camp on Durable Surfaces

- Durable surfaces include established trails and campsites, rock, gravel, dry grasses or snow.
- Protect riparian areas by camping at least 200 feet from lakes and streams.
- Good campsites are found, not made. Altering a site is not necessary.
- In popular areas:
- Concentrate use on existing trails and campsites.
- Walk single file in the middle of the trail, even when wet or muddy.
- Keep campsites small. Focus activity in areas where vegetation is absent.
- In pristine areas:
- Disperse use to prevent the creation of campsites and trails.
- Avoid places where impacts are just beginning.

## Dispose of Waster Properly

- Pack it in, pack it out. Inspect your campsite and rest areas for trash or spilled foods. Pack out all trash, leftover food, and litter.
- Deposit solid human waste in catholes dug 6 to 8 inches deep at least 200 feet from water, camp, and trails. Cover and disguise the cathole when finished.
- Pack out toilet paper and hygiene products.
- To wash yourself or your dishes, carry water 200 feet away from streams or lakes and use small amounts of biodegradable soap. Scatter strained dishwater.

## Leave What You Find

- Preserve the past: examine, but do not touch, cultural or historic structures and artifacts.
- Leave rocks, plants and other natural objects as you find them.
- Avoid introducing or transporting non-native species.
- Do not build structures, furniture, or dig trenches.

## Minimize Campfire Impacts

- Campfires can cause lasting impacts to the backcountry. Use a lightweight stove for cooking and enjoy a candle lantern for light.
- Where fires are permitted, use established fire rings, fire pans, or mound fires.
- Keep fires small. Only use sticks from the ground that can be broken by hand.
- Burn all wood and coals to ash, put out campfires completely, then scatter cool ashes.

## Respect Wildlife

- Observe wildlife from a distance. Do not follow or approach them.
- Never feed animals. Feeding wildlife damages their health, alters natural behaviors, and exposes them to predators and other dangers.
- Protect wildlife and your food by storing rations and trash securely.
- Control pets at all times, or leave them at home.
- Avoid wildlife during sensitive times: mating, nesting, raising young, or winter.

**Be Considerate of Other Visitors**

- Respect other visitors and protect the quality of their experience.
- Be courteous. Yield to other users on the trail.
- Step to the downhill side of the trail when encountering pack stock.
- Take breaks and camp away from trails and other visitors.
- Let nature's sounds prevail. Avoid loud voices and noises.

Other points of etiquette are designed to make everyone's experience on the water pleasant and safe:

1. Obey all navigational rules and park on the launch site policies.
2. Do not encroach on private property. Use public land launching areas.
3. Respect the nights of others on the water. Share the water, avoid inappropriate language and behavior, be discreet and don't interfere with the activities of others.
4. Stay as far away as possible from people who are fishing.
5. Do not harm or frighten wildlife and do not remove plants.
6. Consider supporting area preservation and clean up efforts to maintain the area for everyone to enjoy.

It is every paddler's responsibility to be aware of the area rules and if permits are required. Due to the popularity of the sport, many rivers are attracting more paddlers than can safely be on the river at the same time. Trips must be planned ahead or booked through outfitters who take care of the necessary permission and registration. The most important considerations for open water kayaking are to know the navigation rules and the local patterns of boating traffic.

# First Aid Kits and Medical Considerations

A well-stocked and up to date first aid kit is an essential part of a group's equipment. Items to include are:

- Non-latex rubber gloves
- CPR face shield
- Tweezers
- Razor blade
- Scissors
- Band-Aids and bandages
- Gauze pads and wrap
- Adhesive tape
- Large compresses
- Moleskin
- Thermometer
- Elastic bandages or wraps
- Antibiotic cream
- Calamine lotion
- Hydrocortisone cream
- Bee sting kit
- Burn ointment

- Antibacterial soap
- Antiseptic lotion and wipes
- Lip balm
- Insect repellant
- Sunscreen lotion
- Non-aspirin tablet or ibuprofen

First aid knowledge should include the ability to recognize and handle these likely conditions:

- Minor cuts, bruises and sprains
- Hypo- and hyperthermia
- Head injuries
- Shoulder dislocation
- Shock
- Muscle cramps
- Water in the ear (exostoses)
- Back pain

# Warming Up and Cooling Down

To prepare for a trip in your kayak, it is a good idea to spend a little time performing some simple stretches for each set of muscles, beginning at the head and working down to the toes. These exercises are also good for every-day routines and off season training along with cardio vascular activities such as swimming, bicycling or jogging. To get more out of some elements of your stretching routine, use a paddle or some stationary object for support and resistance. The idea of these movements is to gently stretch your muscles, not to strain them. Use slow, steady pressure for each.

- ***Head and neck*** – Gently lean your ear to the shoulder, using your hand on the same side for additional pressure. Switch to the other side and repeat.

- ***Shoulders*** – Lift your arms straight out from your shoulders and move them in small circles, rotating forward for a while, then backward.

- ***Triceps*** – With one arm over your head, bend it at the elbow to reach behind your neck. With the other hand at your side, bend the elbow to reach up behind your back. Each hand should clasp the fingers of the other hand and gently pull. Switch arms and repeat.

  Another option is to raise one arm up and bend it at the elbow so your hand is touching the back of your neck or upper spine. Use the other arm to gently add pressure to the arm as if to get it to reach farther down your back. Switch and repeat.

- ***Biceps and forearms*** – Extend one arm out straight in front of you with the palm facing up. With the other hand, grasp the fingers and pull on them, keeping both arms straight.

- ***Chest*** – Put your hands behind your back, one hand holding on to the opposite wrist. Keeping the arms as straight as possible, lift your hands alternating hand to wrist positions.

  Another option is to brace your straight arm raised almost to shoulder height and push against the brace while rotating your body away from it. Alternate arms.

- ***Back*** – Cross your straight are over your chest and catch it with the other arm which should be bent at the elbow with the fist up. Use the bent arm to press the straight arm back into the chest. Alternate sides.

- ***Core*** – This demands special attention because it is the source of power and the performance of the most effective paddling strokes. You will be stretching front to back and side to side.

  With your hands on your hips and feet shoulder width apart, slowly bend straight back from the waist while maintaining a normal breathing pattern then lean forward the same way.

  With your hands on top of your head and your feet shoulder width apart, slowly lean to the side from the waist without leaning forward, return to the upright position and repeat on the other side.

- ***Quads*** – Stand comfortably up straight. Keeping your knee pointing to the ground, raise one flexed foot up towards your butt and hold the position. Slowly lower your foot and repeat the procedure with the other foot. Use a support to maintain your balance.

- ***Gluteal Muscles*** – While lying on your back, bend one leg at the knee and raise it to your chest using both hands to apply gentle pressure. Slowly straighten that leg and repeat with the other.

- ***Groin*** – With your legs spread farther apart than shoulder width and keeping you back straight over your center of gravity, place both hands on your upper thigh as you bend that leg so it is bearing your weight. Hold the position, slowly return to the upright position and lunge to the other side.

- ***Hamstrings*** – Without locking your knees, stand with your feet wider than shoulder width, bend forward from the waist and try to grab your ankles (or the back of your legs as far down as you can). Return to the upright position and repeat the process, but alternate between holding each ankle separately after each upright position.

- ***Calves*** – Either starting from a standing position and putting your hands on the ground or from a kneeling position with your hands on the ground in front of you, form an overturned V with straight arms and legs, applying pressure equally over your hands and feet.

- ***Ankles*** – While standing or sitting, extend a leg out so the foot is off the ground and slowly rotate the ankle to perform circles both clockwise and counterclockwise. Switch legs and repeat.

It is also a good idea to test your range of motion in the kayak while wearing a PFD. Perform some simple torso twists and side to side and back and forth stretches. After a day of paddling, cooling off with the warm up stretches helps to prevent stiffness.

# ABOUT THE AUTHOR

Scott Parsons has been a lifelong participant in all types of water sports and camping. Starting with experiences as a Scout then as a leader, outdoor skills were developed and have provided years of enjoyment and excitement. Canoeing and kayaking in local rivers and lakes and camping along the way have been a way of life over the course of years as a guide and for personal pleasure.

Fishing experiences began later on during a variety of trips, both by boat and kayak as well as from pier and shore, in fresh and salt water. The different feelings of peace, excitement and camaraderie are fulfilling and have added tremendous depth to life and interaction with many old and new friends. The wonders of nature feed the soul and the need for the responsibility to protect it is a personal call to action.

Printed in Great Britain
by Amazon

44010930R00061